D0308362

THE BEST WINE RECIPES

THE BEST WINE RECIPES

by Bill Crabtree
edited by Mary Norwak

LONDON
W FOULSHAM & CO LTD
New York   Toronto   Cape Town   Sydney

W. Foulsham & Co Ltd
Yeovil Road, Slough, Berks, England

ISBN 0-572-00936-4

© Copyright W. Foulsham & Co Ltd 1979

All Rights reserved. No part of this publication
may be reproduced, stored in a retrieval system,
or transmitted in any form or by any means, electronic,
mechanical, photocopying, recording or otherwise,
without the prior permission of the copyright holder.

Photoset and printed in Great Britain by
Lowe & Brydone Printers Limited, Thetford, Norfolk

CONTENTS

METRICATION

It is very important to use either the imperial table for measuring ingredients *or* the metric one, and not to mix them when preparing a recipe. The metric scale is not an exact translation of the imperial one, which would be very cumbersome, but the recipes have been tested to arrive at the correct proportions. The metric result is approximately 10% less than that gained with imperial measurements.

The metric scale recommended for British use allows 25 g to 1 oz; and 25 ml to 1 fl oz, instead of the true scale of 28 g to 1 oz. This means that quantities must be 'rounded up' at certain points on the scale, or else vital amounts will be lost as total recipe quantities become larger.

Solid Measures

½ oz	15 g
1 oz	25 g
2 oz	50 g
3 oz	75 g
4 oz	100 g
5 oz	125 g
6 oz	150 g
7 oz	175 g
8 oz	225 g
9 oz	250 g
10 oz	300 g
11 oz	325 g
12 oz	350 g
13 oz	375 g
14 oz	400 g
15 oz	425 g
16 oz	450 g or 500 g
1½ lb	750 g
2 lb	1 kg

Liquid Measures

½ fl oz	15 ml
1 fl oz	25 ml
2 fl oz	50 ml
3 fl oz	75 ml
4 fl oz	100 ml
¼ pint	125 ml
⅓ pint	175 ml
½ pint	250 ml
⅔ pint	350 ml
¾ pint	375 ml
1 pint	500 ml
1¼ pints	625 ml
1½ pints	750 ml
1¾—2 pints	1 litre

When meat and vegetables and some groceries are purchased in metric measure, they will normally be in 1 lb or 2 lb measurement equivalents, and people will ask for .5 kg or 1 kg which is 500 g or 1000 g. When baking, a measurement of 450 g is in proportion with the smaller amounts of ingredients needed.

FOREWORD

Wine making is one of the oldest crafts known to man. Alcohol is produced in nature by the action of sugar upon yeast, and throughout the ages man has made use of this phenomenon, hastened its progress, improved it, and enhanced the flavour and colour to suit his taste.

This book sets out to describe, in simple terms, how, with a very small amount of equipment and a little time, home-made wines can be produced; wines of a pre-determined character and of a measurable strength in either percentage by volume of alcohol or in degrees proof.

There is no doubt that our ancestors produced some very fine home-made wines in their time. The fact remains, however, that these old-fashioned methods and recipes were rather hit-and-miss affairs and the outcome was always in doubt. Sometimes the wine would come out too sweet, sometimes too dry and on the odd occasion quite vinegary – and no one knew why.

The methods outlined in this book will take away all these uncertainties and will explain how you may finish up with the wine of your choice, be it dry red, medium sweet rosé or sweet white. In addition, the book will show how you are able to both control and measure the alcoholic strength of the finished product.

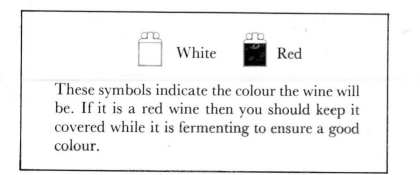

White   Red

These symbols indicate the colour the wine will be. If it is a red wine then you should keep it covered while it is fermenting to ensure a good colour.

BACCHUS

Chapter One

THE REASONS FOR MAKING WINE AT HOME

Most people like to produce things for themselves at home. This urge is to be found in the gardener. It gives a great deal of pleasure to see the results of one's efforts in the garden appearing on the table at meal-times. Besides, the taste of these fresh fruits and vegetables far surpasses that of their counterparts bought from the shop.

The 'do it yourself' enthusiast delights in his work and its results in improving his home. The lady of the house who makes many of her own dresses and coats gets pleasure from her creations. The home decorator can dictate the atmosphere of his home with a cunning selection of colour and decor and the work reflects the personality of the man.

How pleasant it is to be able to produce wine of character for guests at lunch or dinner time! Apart from this, it improves the meal, even if you are dining alone. As a nation we are drinking more wine than ever before, due in some degree to our more frequent holidays on the Continent of Europe, where wine drinking has been a regular habit for many centuries. It is natural to expect a movement to produce our own wine to flourish now, especially since it is so simple and the resulting product so pleasant.

There is no doubt that some people are attracted to the idea of making wine at home simply because it uses up things that would be otherwise thrown away. First of all, there are the surplus fruits and vegetables which all gardens produce from time to time. What a pity to throw them away because you cannot cope with them in the kitchen! Most of them will make good wine. Then there are things which are normally thrown away as a matter of course. Take peapods, for instance. They make excellent wine as do the daily dregs from the teapot when used to make delicious tea wine.

In addition to the ingredients provided by the garden, the countryside furnishes another wide variety. The fields and hedgerows are loaded from early Spring to late Autumn with flowers, fruit and berries. If we need an excuse to spend an hour or two in the country, here it is. At the same time, it is all free just for the trouble of gathering, and all can provide us with the most delectable wines.

Many hobbies in which people get involved are really quite expensive, but here is one which actually pays you for doing it. Wine-making is a very attractive financial proposition. Sugar is the most expensive ingredient which goes into the making, and the cost of up to 3 lbs will represent the main cost to you of one gallon of wine. The small incidental expenditures that are additional to this will mean that each resulting bottle of wine will cost less than 10p. One word of warning here: home-made wine may not normally be sold, although you are perfectly free to make as much as you wish. Without an excise licence it is unlawful to sell the wine you make. There is, however, nothing to prevent you from giving away your wine to friends, and it is worth noting that there is no gift more welcome than a bottle of clear, bright, well-matured home-made wine dressed up to look attractive in a nice bottle with label and foil cap.

Chapter Two

THE BASIC PRINCIPLES

The process employed in making wine has been utilised by man over many centuries. It relies upon the fact that when sugar and yeast are brought together under the right conditions they can produce alcohol and carbon dioxide. The carbon dioxide floats off into the atmosphere while the alcohol remains in the liquid to produce an alcoholic beverage.

To understand how this occurs, it is necessary to know something about yeast. Yeast consists of plant cells which propagate in a sugar solution during a process called fermentation. It is while fermentation progresses that alcohol and carbon dioxide are formed. Alcoholic fermentation can occur between 0 and 50 degrees C, but the best temperature range is 15 °C (60 °F) and 24 °C (75 °F). This, then, is the first condition to be satisfied. When fermenting wine, the aim must be to provide a temperature in this range, or as near to it as possible. It is not difficult to satisfy this requirement in the modern home. In the winter, a warm kitchen, bathroom or airing cupboard will do nicely, while in the summer it is usually warm enough anywhere in the house.

The second condition stems from the fact that yeast requires a slightly acid solution for fermentation and this must be maintained during the fermentation process. This simply means that some little care must be taken in preparing the brew to see that the acid levels are correct. Recipes which show that orange juice, lemon juice or citric acid should be added are ones in which it is necessary to increase the amount of acid present. It all depends upon the nature of the basic ingredient being used. If it is a fruit, then there may well be enough acid present without addition. On the other hand, wines made from flowers will invariably need acid to be added.

During the fermentation process the alcohol content gradually increases, and the amount of sugar in solution is reduced. An instrument called a hydrometer is used to measure how much sugar still remains, how much has been used up, and the alcoholic content of the wine. When the alcohol reaches a strength of about 15 % by volume, the alcohol itself inhibits the yeast and working gradually ceases. The wine-maker who wishes to finish up with a very dry wine must ensure that all the sugar has been utilised before this point is reached. This can be ensured by seeing that the brew is not too sweet at the outset and, once again, the hydrometer is used to determine this. It follows from the above that a strength of about 15 % by volume of alcohol is the maximum that can be achieved in home-made wines. This is so, and it is as well to recall that wine and spirit strengths are usually measured in degrees proof. To calculate degrees proof from percentage by volume it is only necessary to multiply the latter by 1.75(1¾); thus 15 % by volume of alcohol = 26 degrees proof (approx). Having made a wine of this alcoholic strength, it can only be made stronger by the addition of spirit. The spirit most commonly used is brandy and this produces a range of so-called fortified wines. Commercial sherries and ports are all of this kind.

Sparkling wines are different in that they are bottled in very thick, strong glass bottles before the fermentation process is completed. This traps carbon dioxide within the bottle, great pressures are built up and the wine emerges as 'bubbly'. It is not recommended that the novice should begin by making sparkling wines. Special processes are involved and as it will be understood there are considerable dangers from the bursting of bottles. It is not proposed to pursue the making of sparkling wines in this volume.

Chapter Three

UTENSILS AND EQUIPMENT

As a start to a wine-making project, it is suggested that the following equipment would be desirable. Most of these items can be bought from chemists with wine-making departments or from health stores. It will be seen that the necessary items of equipment are both few and inexpensive. Of course, as the project progresses, it will be essential to provide additional storage space in the form of more jars and bottles.

Fermentation jars

Two glass gallon jars will be sufficient to begin with. These jars may be made of clear or coloured glass. The latter are intended for red wines, since if these are stored for any length of time in clear bottles, the beautiful colour will be lost. Daylight affects these wines and gradually the bright red will be turned to dull brown. The coloured fermentation jars are slightly more expensive than the clear ones, but the worst disadvantage is that it is more difficult to see what is going on inside. The problem can be overcome in another way. It is better to protect the wine in the jar by putting a large brown paper bag over it, as shown in the picture over page. The state of affairs inside the jar can be seen easily by simply lifting up the brown paper cover.

As soon as the first two gallons of wine have been started, it will be necessary to buy some more fermentation jars. The wine occupies these jars for several months, for it must be said that one of the main ingredients of wine-making is time. Strong as the temptation may be to try

what you have made, it is as well to resist this urge and attempt to build up some sort of stock. No wine you make will be ready to drink in much under six months from the time you start and even then it will normally improve over twelve or eighteen months or even two years. One popular fallacy is that wine gets stronger in storage. This is not so since the alcohol levels are determined entirely during fermentation. When that ceases the wine can become no stronger, and, as we have seen, that cannot exceed about 15 % by volume. Wine can mature, however, over a period of several years. The wine will improve during this time, will reach a peak of perfection, and if kept beyond that point will tend to deteriorate.

Before deciding upon how much storage equipment to provide there is one other consideration. If you decide to drink on average one large glass of wine each day, one gallon of wine will last about three weeks. This means you will need seventeen gallons to last a whole year. To ensure a continuous supply you will need also to brew at the same rate, that is, about one gallon every three weeks. You should aim to build up to about 20 gallons in glass gallon jars and, as you bottle this into ordinary wine bottles, brew again and so keep the gallon glass fermentation jar in constant use.

For each gallon jar you buy you will also need one single-holed rubber bung and a fermentation lock to fit it. There are several kinds of fermentation lock on the market. The glass ones are somewhat more expensive than the plastic ones and are naturally rather more fragile. The plastic locks are quite adequate although it is not a good thing to attempt to remove them from the bung. In any case there is no need to do so.

Plastic buckets

Two high-density white plastic buckets will be needed to begin the project. These are used for steeping the flowers, fruit or berries that are being used, in order to extract the colour and flavour, and, later on, for holding the wine when it is being poured from the fermenting jar when it is being cleared. One important rule about the equipment should be made here. Except in the first stages, when boiling is called for, no metallic utensils should ever be used. The metal imparts an undesirable taste to the wine. Fortunately, we now have available a wide selection of suitable materials. Glass, white plastic, wood and crockery are all very suitable for the task.

It is necessary to provide sheets of polythene for covering to use in conjunction with the plastic buckets. These should be big enough to allow the polythene to wrap over the edge of the bucket so that it can be secured with a long piece of string round the top lip of the bucket. The covering not only prevents dust and other foreign matter from entering the wine but also excludes the vinegar fly which is capable of turning the whole gallon of wine into vinegar.

Nylon sieve and nylon bag

At several stages during the wine-making it will be necessary to strain the liquid. In order to do this, a sieve and a nylon bag will be found useful. The sieve is for coarse straining and the bag for straining out the finer particles in the later stages.

Gravity hydrometer and float jar

The hydrometer is by far the most important piece of equipment for the modern wine-maker. It is an instrument with which the gravity of a liquid is measured. In wine-making, it is employed to show how much sugar is present in the solution, from which it can be calculated how much has been used in fermentation. This leads on to a determination of alcoholic content. A measure of the growing alcoholic strength, as well as a final figure, can be found. The procedure for using the hydrometer is as follows: the liquid from which wine will be made is called *must*. The must to be investigated is used to fill the float jar to within two inches of the top. The hydrometer is carefully placed into the jar with the heavy end downwards, and the instrument will float. Give the hydrometer a spin to disperse any bubbles that may be clinging to it, which would affect the reading. Now observe the scales on the stem. There will probably be several of these but you are only interested at the moment in the specific gravity scale, which can be recognised by the fact that there is a 1.000 reading near the upper limit. Read off on this scale where the level of the liquid reaches on the stem. Take care not to be misled by the *meniscus*, the distortion of the surface level caused by surface tension.

The correct reading is where the main surface level is likely to meet the stem in the absence of the meniscus. Now in the case of pure water the reading would be 1.000, but when sugar has been added, and is in solution, the hydrometer will be more buoyant. Thus, in one gallon of must to which 1 lb of sugar has been added, the reading will be of the order of 1.040. This is usually recorded by the wine-maker as a gravity of 40, with pure water at 0. The first hydrometer reading is taken when the must has been prepared and the sugar added. This reading will not only depend upon the sugar put in, but also on any sugars which have been extracted from the fruit or other ingredients used. If a very dry wine is required as an end product the initial reading should not exceed 100, otherwise some sugar may be left unused after the fermentation process has been completed – and this will leave the wine sweet. It is also worth noting that a finished wine that is too sweet cannot be made dry, but on the other hand a dry wine can always be made sweeter at the end by the addition of more sugar. The initial hydrometer reading is controlled by the amount of granulated sugar that is added. Normally 2½–3 lb will be needed for each gallon. It is better to add the sugar in stages and take a reading after each addition so that the initial reading can be near to what is desired.

Subsequent hydrometer readings will show how the sugar in solution is being used up. They hydrometer will be less buoyant each time and the hope is that when fermentation finally ceases several weeks later the hydrometer reading will be somewhere between 0 and minus 10. This latter figure is shown on the specific gravity scale as 0.990, and the wine will be very dry.

Alcoholic strength

To find the alcoholic strength of a wine that has finished fermenting it is necessary to know only the initial and final hydrometer readings. Subtracting the final figure from the first will give the fall in gravity that has occurred during the fermentation. This figure divided by 7.36 will show the percentage of alcohol by volume in the finished wine.

Here is a typical example:

First hydrometer reading $= 100$
Final reading $= -8$
The fall in gravity is 108.
Percentage by volume of alcohol: $\dfrac{108}{7.36} = 14.7\ \%$

This table may be used for ready references:

Fall in gravity	Alcohol by volume
50	6.8
55	7.5
60	8.2
65	8.9
70	9.5
75	10.2
80	10.9
85	11.5
90	12.2
95	12.9
100	13.6
105	14.3
110	15.0

The alcohol present in a finished wine is its preservative. To ensure that a wine will keep, the alcoholic content must be at least 10 % by volume. The table will show that to achieve this, the fall in gravity during fermentation must be at least 75.

Most hydrometers show a second scale on their stem. This other scale indicates the alcoholic content associated with a certain gravity reading. Referring to this scale, and by a process of subtraction, the alcoholic content can similarly be determined, as an alternative to using the table shown above. This diagram shows the gravity scale and the alcohol content scale of a hydrometer side by side. Suppose the initial reading of the must is 90 on the gravity scale and the final reading after fermentation is −4. By looking across at the alcohol-content scale corresponding to these readings, it will be seen that the alchohol by volume is 13 % (approx).

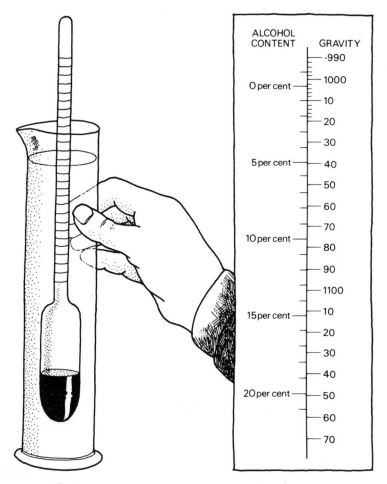

It is usual to express the strengths of wine and spirits in terms of proof spirit. This figure is obtained from % content by volume by multiplying that percentage by 1.75(1¾). Thus:

$$12 \% \text{ alcohol by volume} = \frac{12 \times 7}{4} = 21 \text{ degrees proof}$$

This table will provide a ready answer to this conversion:

% Alcohol by volume	Proof spirit in degrees
10	17.5
10.4	18.2
10.8	18.9
11.2	19.6
11.6	20.3
12.0	21.0
12.4	21.7
12.8	22.4
13.2	23.1
13.6	23.8
14.0	24.5
14.2	25.2
14.6	25.9
15.0	26.6

Siphon

As the wine ferments, and until it has completely cleared, a deposit called the *lees* will be thrown to the bottom of the fermenting jar. The lees, consisting mainly of dead yeast cells, should not be left too long in the wine since it will eventually taint the wine with an unpleasant flavour.

To achieve this, the clearer part is taken from the lees by means of a siphon and an attached piece of plastic tubing as shown in the illustration. The reason for using a

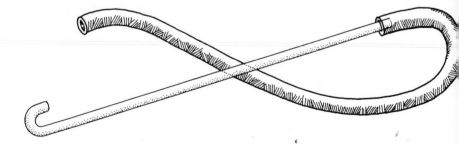

siphon is to cause as little disturbance to the lees as possible while the clearer part is withdrawn. The end of the siphon which is bent up goes into the fermenting jar, while the end of the plastic piece must be below the level of the turned-up portion of the siphon. By sucking on the plastic end, the wine can be drawn through the tube and the liquid will then slowly be siphoned off. The reason for the turned up portion of the siphon can now be seen. Even when the tube is pushed right to the bottom of the jar the bend will prevent the thick lees from being sucked into the siphon. As the level of the liquid falls in the fermenting jar it is advisable to tilt the jar, as shown in the picture. Thus more of the clearer part of the wine can be removed without disturbing the lees. The process by which the clearer part of the wine is separated from the thick part is called *racking*.

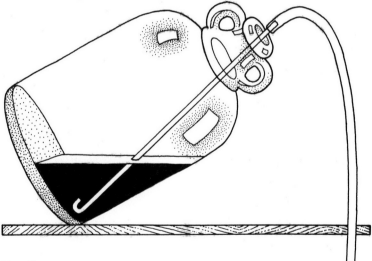

Bottles

It should be repeated that there ought to be no hurry in bottling the wine from the fermenting jar. The wine should be both clear and dry. Then it may be transferred to bottles made specifically for wine. Such bottles can be purchased but really there is no need to do so. Hotels and restaurants serving wines for lunch and dinner throw them away by the dozen and are usually pleased to give a few away. Make sure that the bottles into which you put your wine are, in fact, wine bottles. Spirit bottles are made of thinner glass and should be avoided. There is no possibility, in the case of spirits, that fermentation in the bottle will commence and thus produce pressures in the bottle; but in the case of wine this is not assured. Fermentation can, and sometimes does, start up again, and so wine bottles are made of thicker glass to minimise the possibility of a burst bottle. It is worth remembering that a wine that has been worked out to complete dryness will have in it no free sugar, which must be present for fermentation to start up again.

Wine bottles may be punted or not and this does not matter very much. What is important is that red wine should be put into coloured bottles. The same points can be made as for the fermenting jar. If red wine is put into clear bottles it will not be very long before the beautiful red colour will be lost.

There is one other very important point about the bottles to be used for bottling your wine. Make sure they are always clean and dry. To clean them thoroughly, stand warm water in them to which has been added a heaped teaspoonful of common soda. Leave it like this for several hours, then use the bottle brush and rinse out with clear cold water. The best way to dry out the bottle and sterilise it is to place it in a cool oven. When cold it is ready to fill or store it, fitted with a clean dry cork until it is needed. Never put your bottles away wet or with dirty wet corks. They will be very musty inside when you come to use them if you do.

Labels

Two kinds of label will be found useful. First of all, a tie-on label made from half a postcard will be required,

22

for attaching to buckets and fermenting jars to record the progress of the fermentation. These may read something like this:

TEA

First reading 3-4-74	Started 3-4-74	
12-4-74 Racked.		85
11-5-74 Racked		66
12-9-74 Racked		-8
3-1-75 Finings added		-8
15-1-75 Racked and bottled.		-8
Strength of alcohol	12 per cent by volume	
	21° proof	

The reverse of the label can be used to record anything unusual that occurs, together with a final assessment of the wine.

The second kind of label is for attaching to the bottle in which the finished wine is placed. Many of these stick-on labels are now available from chemists and health stores. They are quite colourful and attractive and add considerably to the finished product.

Large wooden spoon or masher

It is essential to have a very large wooden spoon, or masher, which should be kept solely for wine-making. Metallic spoons should never be used since they may impart an undesirable taint to the wine. Similarly, a wooden spoon that is used for other purposes may also carry over unwanted tastes to the wine. Wine is particularly vulnerable to this sort of thing and seems to readily take on undesirable flavours.

Cotton wool

A supply of unmedicated cotton wool is required for making a loose plug, to put into small bottles containing surplus must in the early stages of fermentation.

Bottle brushes

A couple of bottle brushes will be found useful. First of all a large brush for cleaning out the fermenting jars will be required. A smaller brush will be needed for brushing out the ordinary wine bottles and this will leave only the most stubborn stains for treatment with common soda as previously explained.

Corks

Flanged corks with coloured plastic tops are readily available. These corks can be easily fitted and withdrawn again without the need for a corkscrew. Some people still prefer the long straight-sided cork, but these

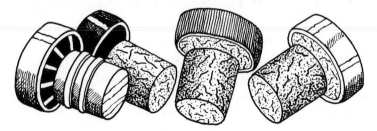

require a special corking tool to force them into place and a corkscrew to remove them. They have little to commend them to the amateur wine-maker. As a final touch to the finished bottle of wine, especially if you wish to present it to a friend, fit a foil capsule over the top of the bottle and cork. These can be bought in many attractive colours and when fitted add considerably to the appearance of the gift.

Miscellaneous

In addition to the above, small quantities of the following substances will be needed. Again they can all be obtained from the chemist who deals in wine-making equipment or from the health store.

Citric acid – Precipitate of chalk. These are both used for ensuring that the must has the correct acidity.

Sodium or **Potassium Metabisulphite.** All wine-making equipment needs washing out with this solution before being used, to destroy the vinegar fly which is capable of attacking the wine and turning it into vinegar.

Campden tablets. These are for sterilising the musts that are produced by steeping for several days in cold water and, later, for stabilising wine before it is eventually bottled. When Campden tablets are not available make a solution by dissolving 3½ oz/100 g/3½ oz sodium or potassium metabisulphite crystals in 2 pints/1 litre/5 cups water (add ⅓ oz/10 g/⅓ oz citric crystals). Use ⅓ fl oz/10 ml/⅓ fl oz of the solution as the equivalent of 1 Campden tablet. This will produce a sulphite solution about 50 parts per million.

Yeast nutrient. A steady growth of yeast activity is required during the fermentation process. Yeast nutrient, added to the must at the time the yeast is added, ensures that this is so.

Yeast compound. Many general wine yeasts are now available and they are very simple to use. Follow the instructions given. About a slightly rounded teaspoonful stirred into the must is all that is required.

Wine tannin. Vegetables boiled without salt are insipid. Similarly wine made without tannin is also insipid. Tannin gives to wine a 'bite', or character. Occasionally, tannin will be present in the ingredients from which the wine is made. This is so when tea wine is made from the dregs of the teapot, but, more often than not, it will be necessary to buy wine tannin and add it at the rate recommended on the bottle.

Pectolytic enzyme. Pectin is found in both fruit and many root vegetables. Pectin forms a jelly when boiled with sugar and this is used in jam-making to enable it to set. In wine-making, however, it can be a nuisance. The pectin can make it more difficult to extract the juices and can also cause the wine to remain stubbornly cloudy. There is a substance on the market which decomposes pectin, thus allowing a more ready extraction of colour and flavour and preventing the cloudiness associated with pectin. It is added to the must during the steeping or soaking process, and a day or two before the sugar and yeast are added. It appears on the market under various names such as Pectozyme, Pectinol, Pectasin, Pectolase or Pectolytic Enzyme. Use it as directed on the packet.

Chapter Four

PREPARING THE MUST

There is an abundant variety of ingredients from which wine can be made. Most flowers can be used to make light, delicately flavoured wines; fruit and berries, full of juice and colour will produce full-flavoured, richly coloured wines; root crops like parsnip, carrot, potato and beetroot can form the base of many delightful wines, although these may take a little longer to come to maturity. For those town dwellers unable to obtain fresh produce easily from the garden or countryside, dried fruit, dried flower petals and even canned fruit juice can be turned into very pleasant wine. It is also possible to buy concentrated grape juice for making both red and white wines. It will prove a little more expensive this way, but a bottle of wine will still be produced at a fraction of the cost of a comparable product bought from the shop.

Before actually beginning to prepare the must, make sure that the utensils you will be using are very clean. First of all make a 2 pint/1 litre/5 cups solution of sodium or potassium metabisulphite by dissolving ½ oz/15 g/½ oz in cold water. Wash out a white plastic bucket with this solution in order to defeat the activities of the vinegar fly. Remember that this fly is capable of completely destroying your wine. This simple procedure of washing with sodium or potassium metabisulphite must be carried out at every stage with every piece of equipment that comes into contact with the wine. For the same reason, the must or the wine should never be left exposed to the air for any length of time at any stage in the making. Cover it with a sheet of polythene when in an open vessel and tie down the polythene with a piece of string.

Having taken these precautions, the task now is to

extract as much colour and flavour as possible from the basic material, whether it is fruit, flower, vegetable or whatever. The procedure for doing this is dictated by the nature of the ingredient being used.

Extraction by boiling

Some very hard materials, such as root vegetables, have to be boiled. These include carrot, parsnip, potato and beetroot. The boiling is continued until the vegetables are quite soft, but care must be taken that at no time does the boiling become too vigorous, since any pectin present may be released to make it more difficult to extract the juices and more likely to produce a wine that is stubbornly cloudy. They should be simmered gently and when the vegetables are soft, strain the liquid off into a plastic bucket. This straining should be done in two stages. First of all, it should be put through the nylon sieve, which is fairly coarse, and then through the nylon bag. When cool add a pectin-destroying agent.

Pouring on boiling water

The most usual way of extracting flavour and colour is simply to pour on boiling water. Do this in a white plastic bucket, stirring well with a wooden spoon or a masher. When cool, add a pectin-destroying agent, following the instructions on the packet. Now cover the bucket with a large sheet of polythene and tie it down securely with a length of string. This is then left for three or four days, the whole being stirred well once or twice daily. As in the previous method, it is now ready for straining. Put it through the sieve, and then through the bag, into a white plastic bucket.

Steeping in cold water

The use of boiling water, as explained in the previous two methods, is too drastic in its action in some cases. It can result in the loss of delicate flavours and essences. The alternative is to steep in cold water and stir daily over a period of several days. Because boiling water has not been used, its sterilizing effect is not present.

29

Consequently, it is essential to add a sulphite in some form to protect the must from infection. The simplest way to achieve this is to dissolve two Campden tablets or add some of the sodium metabisulphite solution to the must, before covering the bucket with a sheet of polythene and securing it with a length of string round the rim of the bucket. At the end of the steeping period, the liquid is strained off as in the previous methods and placed in a white plastic bucket.

The majority of musts are prepared in one of the three methods outlined above. There is just one other variation that is found. In a few instances, it is found advisable to ferment the must in the presence of the pulp. The recipes will make this clear. Fermentation on the pulp will take about seven days, after which the straining is done. The must is then ready to be put straight into the fermenting jar.

Chapter Five

FERMENTING THE MUST

Now that the colour and flavour have been extracted by one of the methods outlined above, the must is prepared for the addition of the yeast. It is already in the plastic bucket where it will stay for the first few days of the fermentation.

The first thing to be done is to test and correct for acid. To procure a steady and adequate fermentation, the liquid must be slightly acid. An experienced wine-maker can tell at this stage, by the taste of the must, whether or not the acidity is correct. The novice should follow the recipe closely, realising that when orange juice, lemon juice or citric acid is to be added, the intention is to increase the acidity. Although it is not essential, the acid content can then be checked by means of special litmus papers, which have been found to be very useful to the amateur wine-maker. They are called narrow range indicator pH papers. They come in the form of a book. One leaf is torn out and dipped into the must to be tested. The leaf colour will then indicate the acidity of the must. By comparing the colour with the chart on the front cover of the book a quantitative assessment of acidity can be determined. Any reading within the limits pH3 to pH5 is acceptable.

In the case of a few fruit wines the natural acid content may be too high and this will show in the finished product. Rhubarb is a case in point. In this wine, it is as well to neutralise some of the acid naturally present by adding precipitate of chalk at the rate of a quarter to half an ounce to the gallon. Again the pH papers will be useful for checking the result.

The must is now ready for the addition of sugar.

Add it slowly, stir with a wooden spoon to dissolve the sugar and measure the gravity with the hydrometer as you go. If a dry, or very dry, wine is being aimed at, the hydrometer reading must not exceed 100. It is not possible to say how much sugar will be needed to reach this point, because of the natural sugars present but it will probably be something like 2½ lb. If a sweeter product is desired, then the reading may be in the region of 120. Whatever the final hydrometer reading, record it now on the cardboard label to be tied to the bucket handle. On the same label will be shown all the subsequent hydrometer readings and the growth of alcoholic content during the fermentation.

There is one final consideration before the yeast is added. Tannin may or may not be necessary, according to the nature of the basic ingredient. Tannin is present in the skins of many fruits grown in this country, but generally our wine will be better for the addition of more. Strong tea at the rate of one tablespoon to each gallon is one way to achieve this. Otherwise, wine tannin may be purchased and used at the following rates:

All wines made from cereals, flowers, roots: 24 drops
All other white wines: 8 drops
All other red wines: 16 drops

The must is now ready for the yeast, assuming that the temperature is correct. If the boiling method has been used for extraction, it is essential to wait until the must has cooled sufficiently. 15 °C (60 °F) to 24 °C (75 °F) is the ideal range. Check with a thermometer and wait for further cooling if the above range is exceeded. Remember that if the must is too hot, the yeast cells will be killed and fermentation will not begin.

Now the yeast nutrient and the yeast may be added. A slightly rounded teaspoonful of each is required. Add it to the must and stir thoroughly with the wooden spoon. Now cover the bucket with a sheet of polythene and secure it round the rim of the bucket with string. Finally place the bucket in a warm place where a temperature of 15 °C to 24 °C can be maintained. In two or three days' time the fermentation will be seen to have begun. Fermentation in the bucket is allowed to continue for four or five days. The early stages may prove quite violent and this is the reason for using an open bucket in the beginning. As soon as this stage is over the must will be ready to transfer to the fermenting jar. The procedure to

• adopt is as follows: using all sterilised equipment, pour the must through the nylon bag and into another bucket. Check the sugar content in the must using the hydrometer. This should be 20 to 30 points below the initial reading. Record the new reading on the card label which was attached to the bucket handle.

The must is now transferred to a fermentation jar, filling it only to the shoulder of the jar, thus giving room for further activity within the jar. Take a plastic airlock and pour in some of the sodium or potassium metabisulphite solution to a height of about ½ inch. Now, pushing this through the hole of a rubber bung, fit it tightly into the neck of the fermentation jar. The card label which was originally secured to the handle of the bucket should now be attached to the handle of the fermentation jar. During this process there is bound to be some must for which there is no room in the jar. Pour this into an ordinary bottle, which has been sterilised, and fit the bottle with a plug of unmedicated cotton wool. Both the fermentation jar and the bottle with the excess must are now ready to return to a warm place where the fermentation can continue. In this, the second stage of fermentation, the process continues in the absence of air, an ideal condition for the production of alcohol. It will continue for several weeks, the evidence of its continuation being the bubbling of carbon dioxide gas through the sodium or potassium metabisulphite solution in the fermentation lock. If a dry wine is wanted as the end product, the final hydrometer reading should be around 1.000 on the specific gravity scale, or a gravity of 0. Sometimes the reading will fall to as low as 0.990 or −.10 and this indicates that the wine is now very dry.

When fermentation ends, the jar need not be kept at the temperature required for that process. Put it aside and the wine will continue to clear and to mature.

On rare occasions, the process of fermentation does not proceed smoothly. It may happen that fermentation begins, the gravity of the must falls 40 or 50 points and then it comes to a halt. It is said to be 'stuck'. There are a number of matters to be considered if this occurs. Has the temperature been maintained at the right level? If not, move the jar into a more suitable place and fermentation should start up again. Was there enough acid present at the outset? Were the lemons too small or lacking in juice? Test with litmus paper and, if necessary, add more citric acid. Stir it well and it may start up again. If these methods do not work, take out about half a pint/250 ml/1¼ cups of the must and add more yeast nutrient and yeast compound to it. Put a cotton wool cork into the bottle and put it in a warm place. When this has begun to work again, add it to the bulk and, hopefully, it will all get going again.

Chapter Six

RACKING THE MUST

At fairly frequent intervals, normally about every four weeks, it is advisable to take off the clearer part of the must from the lees, the thick part which collects at the bottom of the jar. The latter is an accumulation of dead yeast cells, which, if left too long in the wine, will impart an unpleasant taste to it. This process is called racking and is achieved by the use of a siphon, because this allows the clearer part to be removed without too much disturbance of the thick, unwanted deposit.

As the illustration will show, the must can only be siphoned off into a bucket placed at a lower level than the jar from which it is being taken. To begin the process,

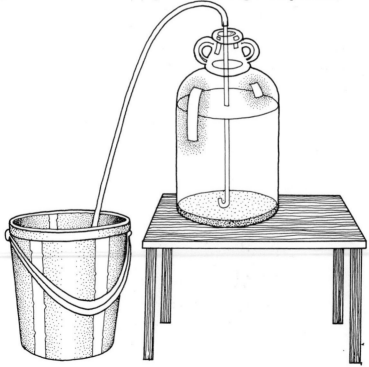

place the glass portion of the siphon with its hooked end into the fermentation jar and into the must. Now suck the wine through, and let it fall into the bucket below. As the level of liquid falls in the jar, make sure that the hooked end of the siphon is well below the surface of the liquid. As the bottom is approached, the jar is tipped forward as shown on page 21 so that as much as possible of the clearer liquid can be removed. Now take a reading with the hydrometer and record it. The fermentation jar should be well washed out and rinsed with sodium or potassium metabisulphite solution before being refilled. Replace the must in the jar. If you have some of the must in another bottle with a cotton-wool bung, use it now to fill up the fermenting jar to the base of the neck. In the absence of any further spare must, fill up the jar to this level with water that has been boiled and allowed to cool.

Chapter Seven

BOTTLING AND STORAGE

At the conclusion of the period of fermentation, the wine will no doubt be cloudy in appearance. Most wines will gradually clear themselves from this point onwards, but the process may be hastened by the addition of wine finings. Follow the instructions given on the bottle and this will normally clear the wine to a sparkling clarity in a matter of a few days. A fluffy sort of deposit will be thrown down to the bottom of the fermentation jar, and again it will be necessary to rack the wine. The lightness of the deposit will bring its difficulties, but it will help if you allow the jar to stand where you expect to rack the wine, for an hour or two before doing so.

The point has now been reached when you should take the final hydrometer reading, calculate the strength of the wine in percentage by volume and obtain a measurement of proof spirit. You will recall that from now on the wine cannot become stronger in alcohol; it can, however, mature and improve in flavour.

The wine may now be bottled off into wine bottles or left for a further period in the fermentation jar. Unless the jar is required for the next brew there is certainly no need to move it out.

Eventually, however, you will wish to bottle your wine. Pour it into a white plastic bucket and dissolve one Campden tablet or ⅓ fl oz/10 ml/⅓ fl oz of sodium metabisulphite solution in each gallon. This will help to stabilise and preserve it. Refrain from adding more sugar at the bottling stage since it may possibly start up more fermentation. Sweetening is best done just before it is drunk. Simply pour the wine into a jug and stir in as much sugar as your taste dictates.

The bottles into which the wine is put must be clean and dry. Above all, there must be no mustiness in the bottle, which might occur in a bottle that has been stored with moisture inside, or with a dirty cork. When full, fit the bottle with a clean cork. The flanged corks with coloured plastic tops are attractive.

The bottle of wine is now ready for its label. Many colourful and attractive labels can be purchased and they certainly add to the appearance of the finished product. The label should state the essential features of the wine: whether sweet or dry, the date it was started, and the alcoholic strength in percentage or proof spirit.

The wine should now be stored in a cool place. The bottles are best kept in a rack which holds the bottles in a slanting position, so that the cork is kept wet by the wine. This prevents the cork from shrinking and excludes the air completely. Also if, by chance, the wine does begin to ferment again, and the cork is forced out, the wine is not all lost as it would be if the bottle had been left on its side.

There is no reason why finished wines should not be mixed. In fact, many wines are improved by blending. Thus if a wine turns out to be too sweet, too dry or too acid, the condition can often by improved by mixing it with another wine.

Chapter Eight

RECIPES

The recipes for wine-making fall into certain groups, determined by the nature of the basic ingredient. Thus flowers, producing wines exquisite in colour, flavour and bouquet, contribute little to the wine apart from these. There is no tannin, no sugar, no acid or nutrient in the basic ingredient to push along the action of the yeast. In wines made from flowers, all these deficiencies must be made up and so, in many respects, the recipes for these wines are similar. In the case of wines made from fruit, the amounts of sugar, tannin and acid from the parent substance vary according to the fruit being used and its state of ripeness. The fact is that these items will be present in greater or lesser degrees and an attempt is made in the recipe to balance them correctly. Pectin is a problem where fruit is concerned and boiling is avoided wherever possible.

Wines made from root vegetables will usually call for boiling until the vegetable is soft. Always simmer gently in such circumstances, since pectin can still supply its difficulties. In these wines deficiencies in acid and tannin will invariably need to be made up. Sugar, however, may be present to an appreciable degree, as, for instance, in beetroot and parsnip in late winter. Care must then be taken to add only enough extra sugar to keep the initial gravity reading to 100, or less if a dry wine is required.

As regards the individual recipes, the following points should be noted:
1.   Where tannin is required, add one tablespoonful of strong tea or use wine tannin from the shop at the rate suggested on the bottle;

2. Many recipes call for a pectin-destroying agent. This appears on the market under various names, of which Pectolase is one. Any of the others will do just as well;

3. Yeast and yeast nutrient, both of which are needed in all recipes, should be used at the rate of one slightly-rounded teaspoonful for each gallon. Make sure the temperature of the must is below 27 °C (80 °F) before adding the yeast;

4. The sugar stated in the recipe is only approximate and, in general, assumes that a dry wine is the objective. Use the hydrometer and add the sugar in stages to bring the initial reading to a value that will produce the type of wine you desire. For a dry wine, limit the gravity reading to 100 on the hydrometer. For a sweeter product, about 120 should be aimed for. For a sweet wine, more body is usually desirable. This can be achieved by introducing up to 1 lb/½ kg/4 cups of chopped raisins and/or crushed wheat or barley to the brew in the first stages;

5. The amounts of water called for in the recipes varies between 7–8 pints/4–4½ litres/17½–20 cups. The ultimate objective is to produce a must of about 9 pints/5 litres/22½ cups. This will be contributed to by the water content of the basic ingredient, which is bound to be considerable in the case of ripe fruit, and by the sugar as it dissolves;

6. Each recipe shows all the ingredients and the method used for preparing the must. The fermentation process, the racking and all that follows is exactly the same in each case and is detailed in the sections of the book dealing with those matters.

Apple

	Imperial	Metric	American
Apples	6—10 lb	2.75—4.5 kg	6—10 lb
Citric acid	1 tsp	1 tsp	1 tsp
Sugar	2½ lb	1.25 kg	5 cups
Cold water	7 pints	4 litres	17½ cups
Campden tablets **or**	2	2	2
Potassium or sodium metabisulphite	¾ fl oz	20 ml	¾ fl oz
Pectolytic enzyme			
Tannin			
Yeast and yeast nutrient			

The apples may include up to 10% crab apples, in which case no tannin need be added. Do *not* use russets. Cooking apples make better wine than eating apples.

Wash the apples and remove the stalk end, the flower end and any rotten portions. There is no need to peel them. Then cut them up into very small pieces, or mince them and place at once into the cold water in a white polythene bucket. Dissolve the Campden tablets or add Sodium metabisulphite to the water. Add pectolytic enzyme and tie a sheet of polythene over the bucket. Leave for up to one week, stirring vigorously twice daily.

Now strain the liquor from the pulp, using a fine nylon bag. Squeeze out as much juice as you can and transfer the strained juice into another white polythene bucket. Add citric acid and test for acidity. Taste it, and, if you think it necessary, use a litmus paper to give a pH reading. Stir in the sugar until dissolved, checking with the hydrometer. Add tannin, yeast nutrient and yeast, cover and put in a warm place to ferment. When the first period of violent fermentation is over, transfer to the fermentation jar.

Apricot

	Imperial	Metric	American
Dried apricots	1 lb	500 g	1 lb
Citric acid	1 tsp	1 tsp	1 tsp
Sugar	2½ lbs	1.25 kg	5 cups
Cold water	8 pints	4.5 litres	20 cups
Pectolytic enzyme			
Tannin			
Yeast and yeast nutrient			

The apricots should be washed well and soaked overnight in 4 pints/2.25 litres/10 cups of water. Then bring to the boil and simmer very gently for 15 minutes. Transfer to a polythene bucket containing a further 4 pints/2.25 litres/10 cups of cold water and allow to cool. Add pectolytic enzyme, cover and leave for at least 24 hours. Now strain through a nylon bag and squeeze it out into a second bucket. Add citric acid and test for acidity. Put in the sugar and stir well until it is all dissolved. Take, and record, a reading with the hydrometer. Add tannin, yeast nutrient and yeast and set aside to ferment in a warm place.

Banana

		Imperial	Metric	American
Bananas	Very ripe, spotted	3 lbs	1.5 kg	3 lbs
Banana skins	or black are best	½ lb	250 g	½ lb
Raisins		½ lb	250 g	2 cups
Lemon		1	1	1
Orange		1	1	1
Sugar		2½ lbs	1.25 kg	5 cups
Cold water		8 pints	4.5 litres	20 cups
Tannin				
Yeast and yeast nutrient				

Peel the bananas and place them, with the skins and the raisins in a saucepan with 4 pints/2.25 litres/ 10 cups cold water. Simmer for 30 minutes. Strain through a nylon bag into a polythene bucket and add a further 4 pints/2.25 litres/10 cups cold water. Allow to cool, then add the juice of the lemon and the orange. Check the acidity and add citric acid if more is needed. Stir in the sugar until it has all dissolved, take a reading with the hydrometer and record it. Now add the tannin, yeast nutrient and yeast; cover the bucket and put in a warm place to ferment.

As variants to the above, use dates, sultanas, currants or mixed dried fruit in place of the raisins. A slightly different flavour will be produced.

Barley

	Imperial	Metric	American
Barley, preferably crushed or rolled	1½ lbs	750 g	3 cups
Raisins	1 lb	500 g	4 cups
Oranges	2	2	2
Lemons	2	2	2
Sugar	2½ lbs	1.25 kg	5 cups
Water	8 pints	4.25 litres	20 cups
Tannin			
Yeast and yeast nutrient			

Obtain crushed or rolled cereal, if possible, because this will save soaking and mincing. Otherwise soak the barley overnight in 1 pint/500 ml/2½ cups of cold water. Wash the raisins and then put the soaked barley and raisins through the mincer. Put this mixture and what is left of the water in which the barley was soaked into a polythene bucket. Add the thinly-pared rinds of the oranges and lemons and the sugar. Take care not to include the white pith from under the skin of the fruit since this will impart a bitter taste to the wine. Pour over 4 pints/2.25 litres/10 cups of boiling water and stir it round to dissolve all the sugar. Now add 3 pints/1.75 litres/7½ cups of cold water and the juice from the oranges and lemons. Test the acidity and add citric acid if more is needed. Make sure that the temperature is no more than 27 °C (80 °F), take and record a hydrometer reading and then add tannin, yeast nutrient and yeast. Cover well and leave to ferment on the pulp. After one week strain through the nylon bag, take a second hydrometer reading and return the must to a fermentation jar. Remember to fill up only to the shoulder of the jar and return it to the warm room to continue the fermentation.

Beetroot

	Imperial	Metric	American
Beetroot	5 lbs	2.50 kg	5 lbs
Raisins, chopped	4 oz	100 g	1 cup
Citric acid	1 tsp	1 tsp	1 tsp
Sugar	2½ lbs	1.25 kg	5 cups
Water	8 pints	4.5 litres	20 cups
Pectolytic enzyme			
Tannin			
Yeast and yeast nutrient			
Cloves ⎤ Optional	8	8	8
Root or lump ginger ⎦	½ oz	15 g	1 tbsp

Clean the beetroots, cut them into 1 in/25 mm/1 in cubes and bring to the boil in 6 pints/3.5 litres/15 cups of water. Simmer gently until the beetroot is soft and turning white. Strain off the liquid into a polythene bucket containing the raisins. Add a further 2 pints/1 litre/5 cups of cold water, allow to cool and put in the pectolytic enzyme. Leave for at least 24 hours, covering the bucket in the meantime.

Now add the citric acid and check the acidity. Stir in the sugar until it has all dissolved and take a reading with the hydrometer to ensure that the quantity of sugar is sufficient to give the type of wine you would like. Now add tannin, yeast nutrient and yeast; cover the bucket closely and put in a warm place to ferment.

Variations on this wine can be obtained by the use of cloves and root or lump ginger, either separately or together. The root ginger needs to be bruised and the spices cooked with the beetroot. This wine, in common with others from roots, should be matured for at least two years. This will allow the earthy flavour and the purple colouration to entirely disappear.

Blackberry

	Imperial	Metric	American
Blackberries	6 lbs	2.75 kg	6 lbs
Sugar	2½ lbs	1.25 kg	5 cups
Boiling water	7 pints	4 litres	17½ cups
Pectolytic enzyme			
Tannin			
Yeast and yeast nutrient			

Place the berries, without stalks, in a polythene bucket and pour on the boiling water. When cool, mash the fruit and add the pectolytic enzyme. Cover and leave for 3—4 days, stirring twice daily. Strain and press the fruit in a nylon bag, collecting the juice in another bucket. It is very unlikely that more acid will be needed, but make the usual test. Use citric acid, if more seems necessary. Stir in the sugar and, when it has all dissolved, take a reading with the hydrometer. Add tannin, yeast nutrient and yeast and put in a warm place to ferment.

Blackcurrant

	Imperial	Metric	American
Blackcurrants	3 lbs	1.5 kg	3 lbs
Sugar	2¾ lbs	1.25 kg	5½ cups
Boiling water	7 pints	4 litres	17½ cups
Pectolytic enzyme			
Tannin			
Yeast and yeast nutrient			

Remove stalks from the fruit before putting it in a polythene bucket. Mash with a large wooden spoon and pour the boiling water over the fruit. When cool add the pectolytic enzyme and steep for 3—4 days, covering the bucket and stirring twice daily. Strain and press, using the fine nylon bag. The high acid-content of blackcurrants will ensure that no further addition of acid will be necessary. Stir in the sugar and, when it has all been dissolved, take, and record, a reading with the hydrometer. Add tannin, yeast nutrient and yeast; cover closely and put in a warm place to ferment. Take care to protect the rich colour of this wine. Keep it from the light throughout.

Broad Bean

	Imperial	Metric	American
Broad beans	4 lbs	2 kg	4 lbs
Raisins, chopped	6 oz	150 g	1½ cups
Lemon	1	1	1
Sugar	2½ lbs	1.25 kg	5 cups
Water	8 pints	4.5 litres	20 cups
Pectolytic enzyme			
Tannin			
Yeast and yeast nutrient			

Use only 'black-eyed' broad beans. Simmer them very gently in 4 pints/2.25 litres/10 cups of water for 1 hour, trying not to burst the skins. Strain into a polythene bucket containing the raisins and add a further 4 pints/2.25 litres/10 cups of cold water. Add the pectolytic enzyme, cover the bucket and allow it to stand for at least 24 hours.

Next day, add the juice from the lemon and test the acidity, adding citric acid if more is needed. Stir in the sugar and, when it has all dissolved, take a reading with the hydrometer. Now put in the tannin, yeast nutrient and yeast; cover over and place in a warm room to ferment.

Carrot

	Imperial	Metric	American
Carrots	5 lbs	2.50 kg	5 lbs
Wheat and barley, crushed	1 lb	500 g	2 cups
Oranges	2	2	2
Lemons	2	2	2
Sugar	2½ lbs	1.25 kg	5 cups
Water	8 pints	4.5 litres	20 cups
Tannin			
Yeast and yeast nutrient			

Clean the carrots, dice them and boil gently in 6 pints/3.5 litres/15 cups water, to which the crushed cereal and the oranges and lemon rinds have been added. When the carrots are tender, strain off the liquor into a polythene bucket, add the remaining cold water and allow to cool. Now put in the fruit juices and test the acidity, using citric acid if more is needed. Stir in the sugar and, when it has dissolved, take and record a hydrometer reading. Finally put in tannin, yeast nutrient and yeast; cover closely and put aside to ferment.

Celery

	Imperial	Metric	American
Celery stalks	4 lbs	2 kg	4 lbs
Lemons, large	2	2	2
Sugar	2½ lbs	1.25 kg	5 cups
Water	8 pints	4.5 litres	20 cups
Tannin			
Yeast and yeast nutrient			

The coarser outside stalks are quite suitable but discard leaves. Cut up the celery and boil it very gently with the thin parings from the lemons in 4—6 pints/ 2.25—3.5 litres/10—15 cups water. When the celery is tender, strain off the liquor into a polythene bucket containing the remainder of the cold water. Allow it to cool, add the lemon juice and test the acidity, adjusting with citric acid if necessary. The must is now ready to receive the sugar. Stir it in well and then take, and record, a hydrometer reading. Put in the tannin, yeast nutrient and yeast, cover the bucket and place in a warm room to ferment. This wine does not carry much colour and you may prefer to use brown sugar to remedy this.

Cherry  or ■

	Imperial	Metric	American
Cherries – any colour, mixed	8 lbs	3.75 kg	8 lbs
Lemons, large	1	1	1
Sugar	2½ lbs	1.25 kg	5 cups
Boiling water	7 pints	4 litres	17½ cups
Pectolytic enzyme			
Tannin			
Yeast and yeast nutrient			

Remove any stalks and then put the cherries into a polythene bucket. Pour on the boiling water and allow it to cool. Now crush the fruit with a large wooden spoon and add the pectolytic enzyme. Cover the bucket and leave it for 3—4 days, stirring the contents twice daily. Strain into another bucket using a fine nylon bag, add the lemon juice and test the acidity. Put in the sugar and stir well until it has all dissolved. Then take, and record, a reading with the hydrometer. Finally add tannin, yeast nutrient and yeast and put in a warm place to ferment.

Clover

	Imperial	Metric	American
Clover blossoms, **or**	8 pints	4.5 litres	20 cups
Packet dried clover flowers	1	1	1
Oranges	2	2	2
Lemons	2	2	2
Sugar	2½ lbs	1.25 kg	5 cups
Boiling water	8 pints	4.5 litres	20 cups
Tannin			
Yeast and yeast nutrient			

Place the clover blossoms in a polythene bucket with the thinly-pared rinds of the oranges and lemons. Pour on the boiling water, cover the bucket and steep for 3—4 days, pushing down the flowers and stirring twice daily. Strain into another bucket and add the fruit juices. Check that the acid level is now correct. Add the sugar, stirring well before taking a reading with the hydrometer. Put in the tannin, yeast nutrient and yeast; cover closely and leave in a warm place to ferment.

Coffee

	Imperial	Metric	American
Coffee, fresh ground	½ lb	225 g	2 cups
Lemons, large	2	2	2
Sugar	2½ lbs	1.25 kg	5 cups
Water	8 pints	4.5 litres	20 cups
Yeast and yeast nutrient			

Pare the lemons thinly and boil the rinds and coffee in 4 pints/2.25 litres/10 cups water for 30 minutes. Strain into a polythene bucket and add 4 pints/2.25 litres/10 cups cold water. Now put in the juice from the lemons and check the acidity. Pour in the sugar, stir until it has dissolved and take a hydrometer reading. Add yeast nutrient and yeast, cover over and ferment.

Coltsfoot

	Imperial	Metric	American
Coltsfoot flowers, **or**	8 pints	4.5 litres	20 cups
Packet dried coltsfoot flowers	1	1	1
Oranges	2	2	2
Lemons	2	2	2
Sugar	2½ lbs	1.25 kg	5 cups
Boiling water	8 pints	4.5 litres	20 cups
Tannin			
Yeast and yeast nutrient			

Place the flowers, with the thinly-pared rinds of the oranges and lemons, in a polythene bucket. Pour on the boiling water, cover and leave to steep for 3—4 days, stirring round and pushing down the flowers twice daily. Strain off the liquor and add the fruit juices, checking then that the acid level is correct. Now put in the sugar and stir it well until it has all dissolved. Take a reading with the hydrometer. Finally add tannin, yeast nutrient and yeast and put in a warm place to ferment.

Cowslip

	Imperial	Metric	American
Cowslip flowers, **or**	8 pints	4.5 litres	20 cups
Packet dried cowslip flowers	1	1	1
Oranges	2	2	2
Lemons	2	2	2
Sugar	2½ lbs	1.25 kg	5 cups
Boiling water	8 pints	4.5 litres	20 cups
Tannin			
Yeast and yeast nutrient			

Pour the boiling water over the flowers and the thinly-pared rinds of the oranges and lemons. Cover and leave to steep for 3—4 days, stirring twice daily. Strain into another bucket, add the juices from the oranges and lemons and test the acidity, adding citric acid if necessary. Now put in the sugar, and, when dissolved, take a reading with the hydrometer. Add tannin, yeast nutrient and yeast and ferment.

Currant (dried)

	Imperial	Metric	American
Currants	3 lbs	1.5 kg	12 cups
Citric acid	2 tsp	2 tsp	2 tsp
Sugar	2½ lbs	1.25 kg	5 cups
Water	8 pints	4.5 litres	20 cups
Pectolytic enzyme			
Tannin			
Yeast and yeast nutrient			

Soak the currants overnight in 4 pints/2.25 litres/ 10 cups of water, then bring to the boil and simmer gently for 15 minutes. Transfer the currants and liquor to a polythene bucket containing 4 pints/2.25 litres/10 cups of cold water. Add the pectolytic enzyme and leave for at least 24 hours. Now strain through a nylon bag and squeeze out as much liquid as possible. Add the citric acid and test the acidity. Stir in the sugar and, when it has all dissolved, take a reading with the hydrometer. Finally put in the tannin, yeast nutrient and yeast and ferment.

Daisy

	Imperial	Metric	American
Field daisy blossoms	8 pints	4.5 litres	20 cups
Oranges	2	2	2
Lemons	2	2	2
Sugar (brown sugar adds colour)	2½ lbs	1.25 kg	5 cups
Boiling water	8 pints	4.5 litres	20 cups
Tannin			
Yeast and yeast nutrient			

Put the daisy heads into a polythene bucket, discarding any green stalks. Pare the rinds of the oranges and lemons very thinly and place these in the bucket with the flowers. Pour on the boiling water and leave it to steep for 3—4 days, pushing down the flowers and stirring at least twice daily. Now strain off the liquor and add the fruit juices. Check the acidity, using citric acid if necessary. Stir in the sugar and when it has all dissolved, take a reading with the hydrometer. Put in the tannin, yeast nutrient and yeast; cover closely and leave in a warm place to ferment.

Damson

	Imperial	Metric	American
Damsons	5 lbs	2.5 kg	5 lbs
Sugar	2½ lbs	1.25 kg	5 cups
Near-boiling water	8 pints	4.5 litres	20 cups
Pectolytic enzyme			
Tannin			
Yeast and yeast nutrient			

Stalk and wash the fruit and place it in a polythene bucket. Pour on the water, which has boiled and been allowed to cool slightly, before being put on the fruit. Pectin is very easily released from damsons and this precaution is taken so that the wine will not remain permanently cloudy. When it has cooled down, crush the fruit, add the pectolytic enzyme, cover and allow it to steep for about 4 days. Stir it round at least once a day. Strain and press the fruit through a nylon bag into another bucket. The liquor should now be tested for acidity, and citric acid used if it is found wanting. Now add the sugar and stir until it has all dissolved. Follow this by taking, and recording, a hydrometer reading. Now add tannin, yeast nutrient and yeast. Stand must in a warm place to ferment.

Dandelion

	Imperial	Metric	American
Dandelion heads, **or**	4 pints	2.25 litres	10 cups
Packet of dried flowers	1	1	1
Oranges	2	2	2
Lemons	2	2	2
Sugar	2½ lbs	1.25 kg	5 cups
Boiling water	8 pints	4.5 litres	20 cups
Tannin			
Yeast and yeast nutrient			

Gather the flowers on a sunny day and make the wine immediately. Begin by removing the heads from the stalks, reducing the amount of the latter to a minimum. Put the flowers in a polythene bucket and add the thinly-pared rinds from the oranges and lemons. Pour on the boiling water and allow to stand for 3—4 days, stirring them round thoroughly twice a day. Then strain off the liquor, through a nylon bag, into another bucket, pressing out the flowers as much as possible. Add the juice from the oranges and lemons and check the acidity, using citric acid if more is needed. Stir in the sugar until dissolved and take a reading with the hydrometer. Finally add the tannin, yeast nutrient and yeast and ferment with a sheet of polythene securely fastened to the rim of the bucket.

Date

	Imperial	Metric	American
Dried dates	4 lbs	2 kg	4 lbs
Lemons	4	4	4
Sugar	1 lb	500 g	2 cups
Water	8 pints	4.5 litres	20 cups
Tannin			
Yeast and yeast nutrient			

Chop the dates and put them into a saucepan with about half a dozen stones and the thinly-pared lemon rinds. Put in 4 pints/2.25 litres/10 cups water, bring to the boil and simmer gently for 30 minutes. A great deal of sugar will have been extracted during this process. Strain off the liquor into a polythene bucket containing ½ lb/225 g/1 cup of sugar. Stir until the sugar has dissolved and then put in 4 pints/2.25 litres/10 cups cold water. When it has cooled to below 27 °C (80 °F), take a reading with the hydrometer and add the rest of the sugar, if necessary, to bring it to the correct initial reading. Now stir in the lemon juice and check the acidity. Lastly add the tannin, yeast nutrient and yeast, and put in a warm place to ferment.

Elderberry

	Imperial	Metric	American
Elderberries, without stalks	4 lbs	2 kg	4 lbs
Lemon	1	1	1
Sugar	2½ lbs	1.25 kg	5 cups
Boiling water	7 pints	4 litres	17½ cups
Pectolytic enzyme			
Tannin			
Yeast and yeast nutrient			

Put the elderberries into a polythene bucket and pour on the boiling water. When cool, crush the berries and add the pectolytic enzyme. Cover over and leave for 4 days, stirring it round twice daily. Strain and press the juice into another polythene bucket. Now add the lemon juice and test for acidity. Stir in the sugar until it has dissolved and take a hydrometer reading. Add tannin, yeast nutrient and yeast and ferment.

Variations in flavour can be obtained by the use of up to twelve cloves and/or ½ oz/15 g/1 tbsp of root or lump ginger. The latter must be bruised by hammering and the spices should be introduced in the first stage, when the boiling water is poured on to the berries.

Elderflower

	Imperial	Metric	American
Elderflowers, **or**	1 pint	550 ml	1 pint (dry measure)
Packet dried flowers	1	1	1
Oranges	2	2	2
Lemons	2	2	2
Sugar	2½ lbs	1.25 kg	5 cups
Boiling water	8 pints	4.5 litres	20 cups
Tannin			
Yeast and yeast nutrient			

Freshly picked flowers, with no green fleshy stems, should be pressed down into a measuring jug. Place the blossoms in a polythene bucket, together with the thinly-pared rinds from the oranges and lemons. Pour on the boiling water and leave to steep for 3—4 days, stirring twice daily. Now strain the liquor through a fine nylon bag, squeezing out as much of the liquid as possible. Add the juice from the oranges and lemons, and make sure the acidity is correct. Put in the sugar and stir it round until it has all dissolved. Now take and record a hydrometer reading, after which the tannin, yeast and yeast nutrient can be added. Cover the bucket and put in a warm place to ferment.

Fig

	Imperial	Metric	American
Dried figs	2 lbs	1 kg	2 lbs
Citric acid	1 tsp	1 tsp	1 tsp
Sugar	2½ lbs	1.25 kg	5 cups
Water	8 pints	4.5 litres	20 cups
Pectolytic enzyme			
Tannin			
Yeast and yeast nutrient			

Wash the figs and soak them overnight in 4 pints/ 2.25 litres/10 cups of cold water. Then bring them to the boil and simmer, very gently, for 15 minutes. Transfer the whole to a polythene bucket containing a further 4 pints/ 2.25 litres/10 cups of cold water. Allow it to cool; then add the pectolytic enzyme. It will now be necessary to let it stand for 24 hours. Strain through a nylon bag and squeeze all the juice out into another bucket. Put in the citric acid and test the acidity. Stir in the sugar and record the reading on the hydrometer. Finally, add the tannin, yeast and yeast nutrient. Cover and put it in a warm place to ferment.

Ginger

	Imperial	Metric	American
Root or lump ginger, dried, well bruised	2 oz	50 g	4 tblsp
Raisins, chopped	12 oz	350 g	3 cups
Oranges	2	2	2
Lemons	2	2	2
Sugar	2½ lbs	1.25 kg	5 cups
Water	8 pints	4.5 litres	20 cups
Tannin			
Yeast and yeast nutrient			

Boil the ginger and the thinly-pared orange and lemon rinds in 4 pints/2.25 litres/10 cups of water for about 30 minutes. Pour on to the sugar and raisins, and add a further 4 pints/2.25 litres/10 cups of cold water. When quite cool, add the juice from the oranges and lemons and check the acidity. Take a hydrometer reading, add the tannin, yeast nutrient and yeast; cover closely and put in a warm place to ferment. Stir round once every day and, after one week, strain and continue the fermentation in a fermentation jar.

Gooseberry

	Imperial	Metric	American
Gooseberries	6 lbs	2.75 kg	12 cups
Citric acid	1 tsp	1 tsp	1 tsp
Sugar	2½ lbs	1.25 kg	5 cups
Boiling water	8 pints	4.5 litres	20 cups
Pectolytic enzyme			
Tannin			
Yeast and yeast nutrient			

The gooseberries should be topped and tailed, and placed in a polythene bucket. Pour on the boiling water, cover and allow to cool. Now crush all the berries, using a large wooden spoon or a masher. Add the pectolytic enzyme, cover again and leave for 2—3 days more, stirring round twice daily. Strain off the liquor and press out the fruit into another bucket. Now check the acidity. If hard, unripe fruit has been used it is likely that very little extra acid will be needed. In the case of soft ripe berries, however, up to one rounded teaspoonful citric acid will be required. Add the sugar, stir it in well and take a reading with the hydrometer. Finally put in the tannin, yeast nutrient and the yeast; cover closely and ferment.

Grape (using fruit)

 or

	Imperial	Metric	American
Grapes, any kind	6 lbs	2.75 kg	6 lbs
Sugar – quantity very variable depending on fruit	1 lb	500 g	2 cups
	(approx)	(approx)	(approx)
Cold water	7 pints	4 litres	17½ cups
Campden tablet, **or**	1	1	1
Sodium (or potassium) metabisulphite solution	½ fl oz	15 ml	½ fl oz
Yeast and yeast nutrient			

Remove the stalks and place the grapes in a polythene bucket with the cold water. Burst the grapes with a large wooden spoon and add the crushed Campden tablet, or sodium metabisulphite solution. Cover over and leave for one week, stirring twice daily. Press through the coarse and fine strainers into another bucket. Grapes usually contain sufficient acid, but test for this, and add citric acid if more is required. There should be enough tannin present and the sugar content of grapes is high, so take a hydrometer reading before adding more. Then add sufficient sugar to bring the initial hydrometer reading to the desired level. The addition of ½ lb/225 g/1 cup of sugar will raise the gravity by about 20. Now add yeast nutrient and yeast and put in a warm place to ferment.

Grape (using grape juice concentrate)

Grape juice concentrates of many kinds are available from shops supplying wine-making equipment. These concentrates are packed either in tins which will make 1 gallon/4.5 litres/20 cups of wine, or in bulk for making larger quantities. In both cases, some instructions for making are usually supplied, but the following notes may be found useful.

The concentrate is simply diluted with water and fermented. For a dry wine, dilute with up to three parts of water to one part concentrate. For a sweeter version, reduce the amount of water in the dilution to about two parts. Check the gravity with the hydrometer; occasionally it will be found necessary to add a little sugar to obtain the correct initial reading.

Making wines from grape juice concentrate will prove a little more expensive than other wines, but they do have one great advantage. They ferment and mature very rapidly and, in many cases, will be clear and ready to drink in two months from starting. The fact remains, of course, that they will further improve when kept longer than this.

Grapefruit (using fruit)

	Imperial	Metric	American
Grapefruit, large	6	6	6
Sugar	2½ lbs	1.25 kg	5 cups
Cold water	8 pints	4.5 litres	20 cups
Tannin			
Yeast and yeast nutrient			

Pare the rinds from the fruit, taking care to leave the white pith behind. Squeeze out the juice, putting it with the rinds into a polythene bucket. Pour over the water and stir round well. The acid level will probably be correct, but check and add citric acid if needed. Stir in the sugar and, when dissolved, take a reading with the hydrometer. Now put in the tannin, yeast nutrient and yeast, cover closely and put to ferment. Stir it round every day and, after the fermentation has been going for 4 days, strain off the must with the fine nylon bag and continue the fermentation in a fermentation jar.

Grapefruit (using juice)

Buy a large tin of unsweetened juice (19 oz/ 500 ml/2⅜ cup) size will be suitable and follow the recipe outlined above, using fruit. Not quite so much sugar will be required if you aim to produce a dry table wine. Try 2 lb/900 g/4 cups sugar to begin with, using the hydrometer to get it right.

Hawthornberry

	Imperial	Metric	American
Hawthornberries	6 lbs	2.75 kg	6 lbs
Lemon	1	1	1
Orange	1	1	1
Sugar	2½ lbs	1.25 kg	5 cups
Boiling water	8 pints	4.5 litres	20 cups
Pectolytic enzyme			
Tannin			
Yeast and yeast nutrient			

Remove the stalks and wash the berries. Put them into a polythene bucket, with the thinly-pared rinds of the orange and lemon, and pour on the boiling water. Leave to cool, then mash the berries and put in the pectolytic enzyme. Cover over and leave for four days, stirring twice daily. Now strain through the coarse and fine strainers, add the fruit juices and test the acidity. It may be necessary to add citric acid. Put in the sugar and, when it has dissolved, take, and record, a reading with the hydrometer. Add tannin, yeast nutrient and yeast, and it will be ready to ferment in a warm place.

Hawthornflower

	Imperial	Metric	American
May blossom (hawthornflowers)	4 pints	2.25 litres	10 cups
Oranges	2	2	2
Lemons	2	2	2
Sugar	2½ lbs	1.25 kg	5 cups
Boiling water	8 pints	4.5 litres	20 cups
Tannin			
Yeast and yeast nutrient			

Put the blossoms into a polythene bucket, together with the thinly-pared rinds from the oranges and lemons. Pour over the boiling water and stand aside to steep for three to four days. It will be necessary to push down the flowers and stir it round twice each day. Strain off now into another bucket, adding the juice from the fruit. Test the acidity. Add the sugar and, when dissolved, take a reading with the hydrometer. Finally put in the tannin, yeast nutrient and yeast and place in a warm room to ferment.

Jam or Jelly

	Imperial	Metric	American
Jam or jelly (mixed if necessary)	4 lbs	2 kg	4 lbs
Citric acid	2 tsp	2 tsp	2 tsp
Sugar	1 lb	500 g	2 cups
Boiling water	8 pints	4.5 litres	20 cups
Pectolytic enzyme			
Tannin			
Yeast and yeast nutrient			

Pour all the boiling water over the jam or jelly in a polythene bucket. Stir well and leave until cool. Add the pectolytic enzyme, cover over and allow it to stand for 3—4 days. Strain into another bucket, add the citric acid and check the acidity. Put in the sugar in stages, checking with the hydrometer all the time, to ensure that a correct initial reading for the sort of wine required is obtained. Add tannin, yeast nutrient and yeast and put in a warm place to ferment.

Lemon

	Imperial	Metric	American
Lemons, according to size	6—10	6—10	6—10
Sugar	2½ lbs	1.25 kg	5 cups
Boiling water	7 pints	4 litres	17½ cups
Tannin			
Yeast and yeast nutrient			

Pare the rind from half the lemons, making sure not to include any white pith. Place the rinds and sugar in a polythene bucket and pour over the boiling water. Allow it to cool below 27 °C (80 °F) before adding the juice from all the lemons, and taking a reading with the hydrometer. Add more sugar if a higher initial reading is desired. Finally put in the tannin, yeast nutrient and yeast; cover over and put in a warm place to ferment. After one week strain and transfer to a fermentation jar.

Lettuce

	Imperial	Metric	American
Lettuce	2 lbs	900 g	2 lbs
Raisins	6 oz	150 g	1½ cups
Crushed wheat or barley	½ lb	225 g	1 cup
Lemons	2	2	2
Sugar	2½ lbs	1.25 kg	5 cups
Water	8 pints	4.5 litres	20 cups
Pectolytic enzyme			
Tannin			
Yeast and yeast nutrient			

Simmer the lettuce for 20 minutes in 6 pints/ 3.5 litres/15 cups of water. Strain off the liquor into a polythene bucket containing the raisins, the cereal and lemon rinds. Add 2 pints/1 litre/5 cups of cold water, cover and leave to cool. Then put in the pectolytic enzyme and leave for 24 hours. After that time, add the juice from the lemons and test the must for acidity, using citric acid if necessary. Stir in the sugar and take a reading with the hydrometer. The tannin, yeast nutrient and yeast may now be added; cover the bucket and put in a warm place to ferment.

Lime Blossom

	Imperial	Metric	American
Lime blossoms	2 pints	1 litre	5 cups
Oranges	2	2	2
Lemons	2	2	2
Sugar	2½ lbs	1.25 kg	5 cups
Boiling water	8 pints	4.5 litres	20 cups
Tannin			

Yeast and yeast nutrient

Take the flowers when fully opened and place them in the sun to dry, in order to bring up the flavour. Then put the blossoms into a polythene bucket with the thinly-pared rinds. Pour over the boiling water and after covering allow to steep for 3—4 days. Push down the flowers and stir them round twice daily during this time. Strain through a nylon bag and squeeze out into another bucket. Add the juice from the oranges and lemons and check that the acidity is correct. Stir in the sugar and, when it has all dissolved, take a reading with the hydrometer. Finally put in the tannin, yeast nutrient and yeast and ferment.

Loganberry

	Imperial	Metric	American
Loganberries	5 lbs	2.25 kg	5 lbs
Sugar	2½ lbs	1.25 kg	5 cups
Boiling water	7 pints	4 litres	17½ cups
Pectolytic enzyme			
Tannin			
Yeast and yeast nutrient			

Remove any stalks from the fruit and place the berries in a polythene bucket. Pour on the boiling water. When cool, mash the fruit and add the pectolytic enzyme. Cover and leave for 3—4 days, stirring twice daily. Strain and press the juice through a nylon bag into another bucket. It is very unlikely that more acid will be necessary, but make the usual test and add citric acid, if more is needed. Stir in the sugar and, when it has all dissolved, take a reading with the hydrometer. Adjust by adding a little more sugar if a sweeter wine is required. The must is now ready to receive the tannin, yeast nutrient and yeast, after which it can be put in a warm place to ferment.

Maize

	Imperial	Metric	American
Maize (or sweet corn)	1½ lbs	750 g	1½ lbs
Raisins	1 lb	500 g	4 cups
Oranges	2	2	2
Lemons	2	2	2
Sugar	2½ lbs	1.25 kg	5 cups
Boiling water	8 pints	4.5 litres	20 cups
Tannin			
Yeast and yeast nutrient			

Soak the maize overnight in 1 pint/500 ml/2½ cups of cold water. Wash the raisins and put them, with the maize, through the mincer. Put this mixture, and the rest of the water in which the maize was soaked, into a polythene bucket. Pare thinly the rinds from the oranges and lemons and put the rinds into the bucket. Now pour 4 pints/2.25 litres/10 cups boiling water into the bucket and add the sugar, stirring it round until it has all dissolved. Add 3 pints/1.75 litres/7½ cups of cold water and, when cool, put in the juice that has been squeezed from the fruit. Test the acidity and add citric acid if more is needed. A hydrometer reading should now be taken, and recorded, when the correct sugar content is confirmed. Add the tannin, yeast nutrient and yeast; cover and put in a warm room to ferment.

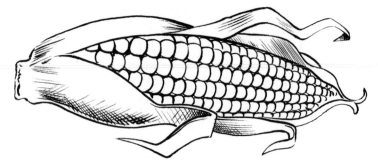

Marigold

	Imperial	Metric	American
Marigold heads, freshly picked	8 pints	4.5 litres	20 cups
Oranges	2	2	2
Lemons	2	2	2
Sugar	2½ lbs	1.25 kg	5 cups
Boiling water	8 pints	4.5 litres	20 cups
Tannin			
Yeast and yeast nutrient			

Place the flower heads, without any green stalks, into a polythene bucket, together with the thinly-pared rinds from the oranges and lemons. Pour on the boiling water and steep for 3—4 days, stirring round the flower heads twice daily. Now strain off the liquor into another bucket, squeeze out the flowers, and add the juice from the oranges and lemons. Check the acidity and correct with citric acid if necessary. Stir in the sugar until it has all dissolved and take a reading with the hydrometer. The must is now ready to receive the tannin, the yeast nutrient and the yeast. Stir round well, cover closely and ferment.

Marrow

	Imperial	Metric	American
Vegetable marrow (or courgettes)	5 lbs	2.5 kg	5 lbs
Root or lump ginger, dried, bruised (optional)	1 oz	25 g	2 tbsp
Oranges	2	2	2
Lemons	2	2	2
Sugar	2½ lbs	1.25 kg	5 cups
Boiling water	8 pints	4.5 litres	20 cups
Tannin			
Yeast and yeast nutrient			

Wash the marrow and grate it, or cut it up finely, into a polythene bucket. Put with it the thinly-pared rinds from the fruit (and the bruised root or lump ginger, if liked). Pour on the boiling water, stir it round and leave to cool. Make sure that the temperature falls below 27 °C (80 °F) before proceeding. Now add the juice from the oranges and lemons and check the acidity. Stir in the sugar until dissolved and then take, and record a hydrometer reading. Add tannin, yeast nutrient and yeast, cover closely and put to ferment. Stir daily and after one week strain and press; then continue the fermentation in a fermentation jar.

Mint

	Imperial	Metric	American
Mint leaves, loosely packed	1½ pints	750 ml	3¾ cups
Raisins, chopped	1 lb	500 g	4 cups

	Imperial	Metric	American
Lemons, large	2	2	2
Sugar	2½ lbs	1.25 kg	5 cups
Boiling water	8 pints	4.5 litres	20 cups
Tannin			
Yeast and yeast nutrient			

Place the mint in a polythene bucket, together with the raisins and the thinly-pared lemon rinds, and pour on the boiling water. Cover and leave for three days, stirring twice daily. Strain into another bucket. Add the lemon juice and check the acidity. Stir in the sugar until dissolved and then take a reading with the hydrometer. Add the tannin, yeast nutrient and yeast, and put to ferment.

Mixed Dried Fruit

	Imperial	Metric	American
Mixed dried fruit	3 lbs	1.5 kg	12 cups
Citric acid	2 tsp	2 tsp	2 tsp
Sugar	2½ lbs	1.25 kg	5 cups
Water	8 pints	4.5 litres	20 cups
Pectolytic enzyme			
Tannin			
Yeast and yeast nutrient			

Soak the fruit overnight in 4 pints/2.25 litres/ 10 cups of water. Then bring to the boil and simmer gently for 15 minutes. Transfer the whole to a polythene bucket containing a further 4 pints/2.25 litres/10 cups of cold water. When cool, add the pectolytic enzyme and leave for a further 24 hours. Strain through a nylon bag and squeeze out as much liquid as possible. Add the citric acid and test for acidity. Put in the sugar, stir well and, when it has all dissolved, take a reading with the hydrometer. Finally add the tannin, yeast nutrient and yeast, cover over and put in a warm place to ferment.

Oak Leaf

	Imperial	Metric	American
Oak leaves	8 pints	4.5 litres	20 cups
Oranges	2	2	2
Lemons	2	2	2
Sugar	2½ lbs	1.25 kg	5 cups
Boiling Water	8 pints	4.5 litres	20 cups
Yeast and yeast nutrient			

The oak leaves should be gathered in early July. Wash off any dust; then place them in a polythene bucket, together with the thinly-pared rinds from the oranges and lemons. Pour on the boiling water, cover over and steep for 3—4 days, stirring twice daily. Strain off the liquor into another bucket and add to it the juice from the fruit. Now check the acidity, adding citric acid if necessary. Stir in the sugar and take a reading with the hydrometer. Put in the yeast nutrient and yeast. Remove to a warm place to ferment.

Orange (using fruit)

	Imperial	Metric	American
Oranges (according to size)	10—12	10—12	10—12
Sugar	2½ lbs	1.25 kg	5 cups
Boiling water	7 pints	4 litres	17½ cups
Tannin			
Yeast and yeast nutrient			

Pare the rinds from about half of the oranges, making sure to keep the white pith behind. Put the rinds and sugar in a polythene bucket and pour over the boiling water. Now allow it to cool before adding the juice from all the oranges. Take, and record, a reading with the hydrometer. Finally, put in tannin, yeast nutrient and yeast and ferment. After one week, strain the must through a fine nylon bag and continue the fermentation in a fermentation jar.

Orange (using juice)

Buy a large tin of orange juice (about 19 oz/ 500 ml/2⅜ cups will do) and follow the recipe outlined above which uses fruit. Not quite as much sugar will be required if you aim to produce a dry table wine. Try 2 lbs/ 900 g/4 cups of sugar to begin with, using the hydrometer to get it right.

Parsley

	Imperial	Metric	American
Parsley leaves, **or**	1 lb	500 g	1 lb
Packet dried parsley	1	1	1
Crushed barley	1 lb	500 g	2 cups
Oranges	2	2	2
Lemons	2	2	2
Sugar	2½ lbs	1.25 kg	5 cups
Water	8 pints	4.5 litres	20 cups
Pectolytic enzyme			
Tannin			
Yeast and yeast nutrient			

Wash the parsley and then simmer it, with the thinly-pared rinds of the oranges and lemons, for 20 minutes in 6 pints/3.5 litres/15 cups of water. Strain off the liquor into a bucket containing the crushed barley and a further 2 pints/1 litre/5 cups of cold water. When quite cool add the pectolytic enzyme and allow to stand for at least 24 hours. Then add the fruit juices and check the acidity. Stir in the sugar until dissolved, and take a reading with the hydrometer. Put in the tannin, yeast nutrient and yeast and ferment, cover closely and ferment. After one week, strain through a fine nylon bag and continue the fermentation in the fermentation jar.

As a variation, this wine can have ½ oz/15 g/1 tbsp of root or lump ginger, well bruised, added in the first stage when the boiling is done.

Parsnip

	Imperial	Metric	American
Parsnips	4 lbs	2 kg	4 lbs
Raisins, chopped	6 oz	150 g	1½ cups
Oranges	2	2	2
Lemons	2	2	2
Sugar	2½ lbs	1.25 kg	5 cups
Water	8 pints	4.5 litres	20 cups
Pectolytic enzyme			
Tannin			
Yeast and yeast nutrient			

This wine is improved by using parsnips which have been well frosted. Scrub the roots and cut away any brown, rusty portions. Cut up the roots and simmer gently in 6 pints/3.5 litres/15 cups of water, until the parsnips are tender. Strain off the liquor on to the raisins and thinly-pared rinds in a polythene bucket. Add 2 pints/1 litre/5 cups of cold water and, when quite cold, put in the pectolytic enzyme. Cover and leave for 24 hours. Now add the juice from the oranges and lemons and test for acidity. Stir in the sugar until dissolved, and take a hydrometer reading. Add tannin, yeast nutrient and yeast and put into a warm place to ferment.

Peach

	Imperial	Metric	American
Ripe peaches	3 lbs	1.5 kg	3 lbs
Citric acid	2 tsp	2 tsp	2 tsp
Sugar	2½ lbs	1.25 kg	5 cups
Boiling water	7 pints	4 litres	17½ cups
Pectolytic enzyme			
Tannin			
Yeast and yeast nutrient			

Wipe the peaches, take out the stones and place the fruit in a polythene bucket. Pour on the boiling water and mash the peaches with a large wooden spoon. Leave overnight and add the pectolytic enzyme. After three more days, strain and press out the juice into another polythene bucket. Add the citric acid and test for acidity. Now stir in the sugar until dissolved, and take a reading with the hydrometer. Finally add tannin, yeast nutrient and yeast and put in a warm place to ferment.

Pea Pod

	Imperial	Metric	American
Pea pods	5 lbs	2.5 kg	5 lbs
Citric acid	2 tsp	2 tsp	2 tsp
Sugar	2½ lbs	1.25 kg	5 cups
Water	8 pints	4.5 litres	20 cups
Pectolytic enzyme			
Tannin			
Yeast and yeast nutrient			

The pea pods should be clean and fresh. Boil them very gently in the water until they are tender. Strain off the liquor and when cool add the pectolytic enzyme. Leave for 24 hours. Now add the citric acid and test for acidity. Stir in the sugar and, when completely dissolved, take and record a hydrometer reading. Add tannin, yeast nutrient and yeast and ferment.

Pear

	Imperial	Metric	American
Pears	6 lbs	2.75 kg	6 lbs
Lemons, large	2	2	2
Sugar	2½ lbs	1.25 kg	5 cups
Boiling water	8 pints	4.5 litres	20 cups
Pectolytic enzyme			
Yeast and yeast nutrient			

Wipe the fruit, cut it up to include pips and skin, and put it into a polythene bucket. Pour on the boiling water and leave to cool before adding the pectolytic enzyme. Now cover it and allow it to stand for 3—4 days, mashing and stirring twice daily. Then strain off the liquor into another bucket, using the coarse and fine strainers. Add the lemon juice and check the acidity, using citric acid if more is needed. Stir in the sugar and, when it has all dissolved, take a reading with the hydrometer. The must is now ready to receive the yeast nutrient and the yeast. Tannin should not be necessary since it exists under the skins of pears and this should be adequate. Now put in a warm place to ferment.

Pineapple (using fruit)

	Imperial	Metric	American
Pineapples, medium size	4	4	4
Lemons	2	2	2
Sugar	2½ lbs	1.25 kg	5 cups
Water	8 pints	4.5 litres	20 cups
Pectolytic enzyme			
Tannin			
Yeast and yeast nutrient			

Cut off the tops from the pineapples, then slice them up into a large saucepan. Pour on 6 pints/3.5 litres/ 15 cups of water, bring to the boil and simmer very gently for about 20 minutes. Strain off the liquor into a polythene bucket containing a further 2 pints/1 litre/5 cups of cold water, allow it to cool and add the pectolytic enzyme. Cover the bucket and set it aside for at least 24 hours. Now add the juice of the lemons and check the acidity, using citric acid if it seems necessary. Stir in the sugar and, when dissolved, take a hydrometer reading. Finally add tannin, yeast nutrient and yeast and put in a warm place to ferment.

Pineapple (using juice)

As in the case of orange and grapefruit, wine can be made from pineapple juice. To make 8 pints/4.5 litres/20 cups of pineapple wine, you will need two 19 oz/500 ml/ 2⅜ cups (or one 43 oz tin) of juice. Follow the recipe outline above, which uses fruit. It is likely that 2 lbs/900 g/4 cups sugar will be sufficient. Try this amount first and use the hydrometer to get it right.

Pink or Carnation

	Imperial	Metric	American
Carnation or Pink heads	4 pints	2.25 litres	10 cups
Oranges	2	2	2
Lemons	2	2	2
Sugar	2½ lbs	1.25 kg	5 cups
Boiling water	8 pints	4.5 litres	20 cups
Tannin			
Yeast and yeast nutrient			

Place the flower heads into a polythene bucket, together with the thinly-pared rinds of the oranges and lemons. Pour on the boiling water and steep for 3—4 days. Cover the bucket and stir the heads round twice each day. Then strain off the liquid through a nylon bag, pressing out as much from the flowers as possible. Add the juice from the oranges and lemons and check that the acidity is correct. Add the sugar and stir well to ensure that it completely dissolves. Take, and record a reading with the hydrometer. Now put in the tannin, yeast nutrient and the yeast and put in a warm room to ferment.

Plum

 or

	Imperial	Metric	American
Plums	6 lbs	2.75 kg	6 lbs
Sugar	2½ lbs	1.25 kg	5 cups
Water, nearly boiling	8 pints	4.5 litres	20 cups
Pectolytic enzyme			
Tannin			
Yeast and yeast nutrient			

Remove any stalks from the plums, wash them and place into a polythene bucket. Pour on to them the water, which has boiled and then been allowed to cool a little. Pectin is very easily released from plums and every effort must be made to prevent the wine from becoming permanently cloudy. When quite cool, mash the fruit and add the pectolytic enzyme. Cover the bucket and allow it to stand for 3—4 days, stirring round twice daily. Strain and press the fruit through a nylon bag into another bucket. The liquor should now be tested for correct acidity, and, if necessary, citric acid added. Put in the sugar and stir until it has all dissolved. Now take a reading with the hydrometer, ensuring that the sugar quantity registered on the initial reading will produce the type of wine required. Add tannin, yeast nutrient and yeast and ferment.

Potato

	Imperial	Metric	American
Potatoes	5 lbs	2.25 kg	5 lbs
Raisins, chopped	12 oz	350 g	3 cups
Crushed wheat or barley	1 lb	500 g	2 cups
Lemons, large	2	2	2
Sugar	2½ lbs	1.25 kg	5 cups
Water	8 pints	4.5 litres	20 cups
Pectolytic enzyme			
Tannin			
Yeast and yeast nutrient			

There is no need to peel the potatoes, but remove any discoloured parts and cut them up into a large saucepan. Boil the potatoes slowly in 6—8 pints/ 3.5—4.5 litres/17½—20 cups of water until they are just tender. Strain off the liquor into a polythene bucket containing the raisins and the crushed cereal and then make up the water used to 8 pints/4.5 litres/20 cups. Allow the whole to cool and add the pectolytic enzyme. Leave for at least 24 hours; then add the lemon juice and test the acidity. Stir in the sugar and check the gravity, using the hydrometer. Now put in tannin, yeast nutrient and yeast and put in a warm room to ferment.

Primrose

	Imperial	Metric	American
Fresh primroses	8 pints	4.5 litres	20 cups
Oranges	2	2	2
Lemons	2	2	2
Sugar	2½ lbs	1.25 kg	5 cups
Boiling water	8 pints	4.5 litres	20 cups
Tannin			
Yeast and yeast nutrient			

Place the flowers, without any stalks, into a polythene bucket containing the thinly-pared rinds of the oranges and lemons. Pour on the boiling water and leave to steep for 3—4 days. Cover the bucket and stir round the contents twice daily. Strain off into another bucket and add the juice from the fruit. Test the acidity and correct with citric acid if necessary. Stir in the sugar and take a reading with the hydrometer. Finally add tannin, yeast nutrient and yeast and ferment.

Raisin

	Imperial	Metric	American
Raisins	4 lbs	2 kg	16 cups
Citric acid	2 tsp	2 tsp	2 tsp
Sugar	1 lb	500 g	2 cups
Water	8 pints	4.5 litres	20 cups
Pectolytic enzyme			
Tannin			
Yeast and yeast nutrient			

Soak the raisins overnight in 4 pints/2.25 litres/ 10 cups of water. Then bring the fruit to the boil and simmer very gently for 15 minutes. Transfer the whole to a polythene bucket, which has in it the remaining 4 pints/ 2.25 litres/10 cups of cold water. When quite cold, put in the pectolytic enzyme and allow it to stand for at least 24 hours. Strain through a nylon bag, squeezing out as much of the liquid as possible. Add the citric acid and test for acidity. Now put in the sugar and stir it round so that it all dissolves. Take a hydrometer reading and check that the lower than usual amount of sugar has been sufficient to bring the initial gravity reading to a suitable level. Add more sugar, if it seems necessary. Put in the tannin, yeast nutrient and yeast and ferment.

Raspberry

	Imperial	Metric	American
Raspberries	2½ lbs	1.25 kg	2½ lbs
Raisins	½ lb	225 g	2 cups
Sugar	2½ lbs	1.25 kg	5 cups
Boiling water	7 pints	4 litres	17½ cups
Pectolytic enzyme			
Tannin			
Yeast and yeast nutrient			

Remove any stalks from the fruit and put it into a polythene bucket. Pour over the boiling water and leave to cool. Mash the fruit well and then put in the pectolytic enzyme. Cover the bucket and allow it to steep for 3—4 days, stirring the contents twice daily. At the end of that time, strain and press the fruit through a nylon bag into another polythene bucket. The acidity will probably be correct, but make the usual test to be sure. Now stir in the sugar until it has quite dissolved and take a reading with the hydrometer. Make any adjustments to obtain a suitable initial reading. Put in the tannin, yeast nutrient and yeast and put in a warm room to ferment.

Redcurrant

	Imperial	Metric	American
Redcurrants	5 lbs	2.25 kg	5 lbs
Sugar	2½ lbs	1.25 kg	5 cups
Boiling water	7 pints	4 litres	17½ cups
Pectolytic enzyme			
Tannin			
Yeast and yeast nutrient			

Make sure all the stalks have been removed from the currants; then put the fruit into a polythene bucket. Pour on the boiling water, allow to cool, and then mash the fruit with a masher or a large wooden spoon. When quite cold, put in the pectolytic enzyme, cover the bucket and allow it to steep for 3—4 days. During this time, stir the fruit round twice a day. Then put through a nylon bag and into another bucket. Press out as much of the liquid as possible. It is very unlikely that more acid will be needed, but make the usual acidity test. Now stir in the sugar and, when it has completely dissolved, take a reading with the hydrometer. Add the tannin, yeast nutrient and yeast and ferment.

Rhubarb

	Imperial	Metric	American
Rhubarb	6 lbs	2.75 kg	6 lbs
Precipitate of chalk	½ oz	15 g	½ oz
Sugar	2½ lbs	1.25 kg	5 cups
Cold water	7 pints	4 litres	17½ cups
Campden tablet, **or**	1	1	1
Sodium metabisulphite solution	⅓ fl oz	10 ml	⅓ fl oz
Tannin			
Yeast and yeast nutrient			

The rhubarb is best picked at the end of May for making wine. Wipe each stick; then cut it up and put it into a polythene bucket. Do not remove the skin, since it will help to colour the wine. Pour on the water and put in the crushed Campden tablet, or sodium (or potassium) metabisulphite solution. Cover over and allow it to steep for 3—4 days. During this time, stir round twice daily and break up the fruit as much as possible to release the juice. Strain off the liquor, and squeeze out as much juice as possible from the fruit. Because rhubarb is so rich in acid, it will no doubt be necessary to neutralize some of it with precipitate of chalk. Mix ¼ oz/7 g/¼ oz to a smooth paste and stir it into the must. Foaming will occur; when it has subsided, test with pH litmus paper. Add a further ¼ oz/7 g/¼ oz of precipitate of chalk, or less, if it seems necessary, to achieve the desired acid level between pH3 and pH5. Now add the sugar and stir it in until dissolved. Take, and record, a reading with the hydrometer. The must is now ready to receive the tannin, yeast nutrient and yeast; afterwards put into warm place to ferment.

Rhubarb is a very suitable ingredient for mixing with others and this can eliminate one of the problems of rhubarb, namely, the excess acid.

Rose Hip

	Imperial	Metric	American
Rose hips	3½ lbs	1.5 kg	3½ lbs
Citric acid	2 tsps	2 tsps	2 tsps
Sugar	2½ lbs	1.25 kg	5 cups
Boiling water	8 pints	4.5 litres	20 cups
Tannin			
Yeast and yeast nutrient			

Remove all the stalks from the rose hips. Wash the hips and place them in a polythene bucket. Pour on the boiling water and stir in the sugar. Allow to cool to below 27 °C (80 °F) and then add the citric acid, tannin, yeast nutrient and yeast. Take, and record, the initial hydrometer reading; then put the bucket into a warm room and ferment on the pulp. After one week, strain through the coarse and fine strainers and transfer the must to the fermentation jar to continue the process.

Rose Petal

	Imperial	Metric	American
Rose petals, strongly scented	4 pints	2.25 litres	10 cups
Oranges	2	2	2
Lemons	2	2	2
Sugar	2½ lbs	1.25 kg	5 cups
Boiling water	8 pints	4.5 litres	20 cups
Tannin			
Yeast and yeast nutrient			

Place the rose petals, and the thinly-pared rinds of the oranges and lemons, into a bucket. Pour on the boiling water and leave to steep for 3—4 days, stirring round and pushing down the flowers twice daily. Strain off the liquor and add the fruit juices, checking that the acid level is correct. Now put in the sugar and stir it well until it has all dissolved. Take a reading with the hydrometer and record it. Finally add the tannin, yeast nutrient and yeast and put into a warm room to ferment.

Rowanberry

	Imperial	Metric	American
Rowanberries	5 lbs	2.25 kg	5 lbs
Crushed wheat or barley	½ lb	225 g	1 cup
Raisins, chopped	6 oz	150 g	1½ cups
Orange	1	1	1
Lemon	1	1	1
Sugar	2½ lbs	1.25 kg	5 cups
Boiling water	8 pints	4.5 litres	20 cups
Pectolytic enzyme			
Tannin			
Yeast and yeast nutrient			

Remove all the stalks and wash the berries. Put them into a polythene bucket together with the crushed cereal, the raisins and the thinly-pared rinds of the orange and lemon. Pour over the boiling water and allow to cool before putting in the pectolytic enzyme. Cover the bucket and leave to steep for 3—4 days, stirring it round twice each day. Strain the liquor off into another bucket. Use the coarse and fine strainers and squeeze out as much liquid as possible. Now add the fruit juices and test the acidity, using citric acid if more seems necessary. Put in the sugar and stir round well until it has all dissolved. Take, and record, a reading with the hydrometer. Add the tannin, yeast nutrient and yeast and put into a warm room to ferment.

Sloe

	Imperial	Metric	American
Sloes	2½ lbs	1.25 kg	2½ lbs
Sugar	2½ lbs	1.25 kg	5 cups
Boiling water	8 pints	4.5 litres	20 cups
Pectolytic enzyme			
Yeast and yeast nutrient			

Sloes should be picked when fully ripe, preferably in November. They are high in acid and tannin, and should not need these additions.

Remove the stalks and place the sloes in a polythene bucket. Pour on the boiling water, and leave to cool before putting in the pectolytic enzyme. Cover the bucket and leave to steep for 3—4 days, stirring the contents twice daily. Strain off the liquor, and squeeze out the berries as much as possible. Now just test the acidity to make sure it it is correct. Stir in the sugar and, when dissolved, take a reading with the hydrometer and record it on the label. Finally, add the yeast nutrient and the yeast and put into a warm place to ferment.

Strawberry

	Imperial	Metric	American
Strawberries	6 lbs	2.75 kg	6 lbs
Boiling water	7 pints	4 litres	17½ cups
Sugar	2½ lbs	1.25 kg	5 cups
Tannin			
Yeast and yeast nutrient			

Place the strawberries into a polythene bucket, having removed any stalks. Pour on the boiling water and, when cool, mash the berries with a large wooden spoon or masher. Pectolytic enzyme is not necessary since strawberries are very low in pectin. Cover and leave for 3—4 days, stirring round thoroughly twice daily. Strain, and press the juice through a nylon bag into another bucket. It is not likely that more acid will be needed, but make the usual test to be quite sure. Now stir in the sugar, and take a hydrometer reading. Add tannin, yeast nutrient and yeast and ferment.

Tangerine

	Imperial	Metric	American
Tangerines	15	15	15
Sugar	2½ lbs	1.25 kg	5 cups
Boiling water	7 pints	4 litres	17½ cups
Tannin			
Yeast and yeast nutrient			

Pare the rind from half of the tangerines, taking care not to include any of the white pith. Place the rinds and the sugar into a polythene bucket and pour on the boiling water. Allow it to cool before adding the juice from all the tangerines; then take a reading with the hydrometer. Finally, put in the tannin, the yeast nutrient and the yeast and ferment.

Tea

	Imperial	Metric	American
Tea, very weak	8 pints	4.5 litres	20 cups
Raisins, chopped	1 lb	500 g	4 cups
Oranges	2	2	2
Lemons	2	2	2
Sugar	2½ lbs	1.25 kg	5 cups
Yeast and yeast nutrient			

Dregs from the teapot, if put aside for a couple of days, will usually provide the tea for this wine. It must be stressed that only very weak tea is needed and tea from the pot will need watering down very considerably, say, 1 pint/500 ml/2½ cups of tea to make 8 pints/4.5 litres/20 cups. Place the weak tea in a polythene bucket and add the raisins and the rinds and juice of the oranges and lemons. Test for acidity. Stir in the sugar until dissolved, and then take a reading with the hydrometer. Add yeast nutrient and yeast and ferment.

Chapter Nine

POINTS TO BEAR IN MIND WHEN THINGS GO WRONG!

1. When fermentation does not begin.
   (a) Check that the temperature is within the range 15 °C (60 °F) to 24 °C (75 °F). Moving the must to a warmer place will sometimes solve the problem.
   (b) The yeast may be old and dead. Try a different sample of yeast.
2. When fermentation starts, but stops too soon. The brew becomes 'stuck' at a gravity reading of, say, 40 to 60. Withdraw ½ pint/250 ml/1¼ cups of the must into a small bottle, and add to this one level teaspoonful of yeast nutrient and yeast compound. Put a cotton-wool bung into the bottle and place it in a warm place 15 °C (60 °F) to 24 °C (75 °F). When the must has begun to work again, add it to the bulk and it should all get going again.
3. If it turns vinegary, I am afraid your sterilization procedure has failed. It could only have been prevented by a stricter use of the sodium or potassium metabisulphite solution, which keeps the vinegar fly at bay. Wine which has been thus attacked cannot be saved. Either throw it away or find some use for it as wine vinegar.
4. If the wine has fermented out to zero gravity and shows no sign of clearing after a month or so, this process can be hastened by adding wine finings at the rate stated on the bottle or packet. This will improve the wine to a sparkling clearness in a matter of days. Of course you will have to rack the wine again as the deposit falls to the bottom of the bottle.

INDEX